A PHOENIX
TOO FREQUENT

'To whom conferr'd a peacock's undecent,
A squirrel's harsh, a phoenix too frequent.'

ROBERT BURTON QUOTING MARTIAL

CHRISTOPHER FRY

A PHOENIX
TOO FREQUENT

A COMEDY

Illustrated by Ronald Searle

LONDON
OXFORD UNIVERSITY PRESS
NEW YORK   TORONTO
1959

Oxford University Press, Amen House, London E.C.4

GLASGOW NEW YORK TORONTO MELBOURNE WELLINGTON
BOMBAY CALCUTTA MADRAS KARACHI KUALA LUMPUR
CAPE TOWN IBADAN NAIROBI ACCRA

First published by Hollis & Carter 1946
Reissued by the Oxford University Press 1949
Second impression (reset) 1949, reprinted 1950, 1951,
1952, 1953, and 1955
First published in this edition 1959

PRINTED IN GREAT BRITAIN

CHARACTERS

DYNAMENE

DOTO

TEGEUS—CHROMIS

SCENE

The tomb of Virilius, near Ephesus; night

NOTE

The story was got from Jeremy Taylor who
had it from Petronius

TO
MY WIFE

A PHOENIX TOO FREQUENT

First produced at the Mercury Theatre, London
25 April 1946

Dynamene	HERMIONE HANNEN
Doto	ELEANOR SUMMERFIELD
Tegeus-Chromis	ALAN WHEATLEY

Directed by E. Martin Browne

Revived at the Arts Theatre, London
20 November 1946

Dynamene	HERMIONE HANNEN
Doto	JOAN WHITE
Tegeus-Chromis	PAUL SCOFIELD

Directed by Noël Willman

A PHOENIX TOO FREQUENT

An underground tomb, in darkness except for the very low light of an oil-lamp. Above ground the starlight shows a line of trees on which hang the bodies of several men. It also penetrates a gate and falls on to the first of the steps which descend into the darkness of the tomb. DOTO *talks to herself in the dark.*

DOTO

Nothing but the harmless day gone into black
Is all the dark is. And so what's my trouble?
Demons is so much wind. Are so much wind.
I've plenty to fill my thoughts. All that I ask
Is don't keep turning men over in my mind,
Venerable Aphrodite. I've had my last one
And thank you. I thank thee. He smelt of sour grass
And was likeable. He collected ebony quoits.

　　　　　　　　　　　　[*An owl hoots near at hand.*

O Zeus! O some god or other, where is the oil?

Fire's from Prometheus. I thank thee. If I
Mean to die I'd better see what I'm doing.

> [*She fills the lamp with oil. The flame burns up brightly and shows* DYNAMENE, *beautiful and young, leaning asleep beside a bier.*

Honestly, I would rather have to sleep
With a bald bee-keeper who was wearing his boots
Than spend more days fasting and thirsting and crying
In a tomb. I shouldn't have said that. Pretend
I didn't hear myself. But life and death
Is cat and dog in this double-bed of a world.
My master, my poor master, was a man
Whose nose was as straight as a little buttress,
And now he has taken it into Elysium
Where it won't be noticed among all the other straightness.

> [*The owl cries again and wakens* DYNAMENE.

Oh, them owls. Those owls. It's woken her.

DYNAMENE

Ah! I'm breathless. I caught up with the ship
But it spread its wings, creaking a cry of *Dew*,
Dew! and flew figurehead foremost into the sun.

DOTO

How crazy, madam.

DYNAMENE

Doto, draw back the curtains.
I'll take my barley-water.

DOTO

We're not at home
Now, madam. It's the master's tomb.

[2]

DYNAMENE

Of course!
Oh, I'm wretched. Already I have disfigured
My vigil. My cynical eyelids have soon dropped me
In a dream.

DOTO

But then it's possible, madam, you might
Find yourself in bed with him again
In a dream, madam. Was he on the ship?

DYNAMENE

He was the ship.

DOTO

Oh. That makes it different.

DYNAMENE

He was the ship. He had such a deck, Doto,
Such a white, scrubbed deck. Such a stern prow,
Such a proud stern, so slim from port to starboard.
If ever you meet a man with such fine masts
Give your life to him, Doto. The figurehead
Bore his own features, so serene in the brow
And hung with a little seaweed. O Virilius,
My husband, you have left a wake in my soul.
You cut the glassy water with a diamond keel.
I must cry again.

DOTO

What, when you mean to join him?
Don't you believe he will be glad to see you, madam?
Thankful to see you, I should imagine, among
Them shapes and shades; all shapes of shapes and all

[3]

Shades of shades, from what I've heard. I know
I shall feel odd at first with Cerberus,
Sop or no sop. Still, I know how you feel, madam.
You think he may find a temptation in Hades.
I shouldn't worry. It would help him to settle down.

[DYNAMENE *weeps.*

It would only be *fun*, madam. He couldn't go far
With a shade.

DYNAMENE

He was one of the coming men.
He was certain to have become the most well-organized provost
The town has known, once they had made him provost.
He was so punctual, you could regulate
The sun by him. He made the world succumb
To his daily revolution of habit. But who,

[4]

In the world he has gone to, will appreciate that?
O poor Virilius! To be a coming man
Already gone—it must be distraction.
Why did you leave me walking about our ambitions
Like a cat in the ruins of a house? Promising husband,
Why did you insult me by dying ? Virilius,
Now I keep no flower, except in the vase
Of the tomb.

DOTO

O poor madam! O poor master!
I presume so far as to cry somewhat for myself
As well. I know you won't mind, madam. It's two
Days not eating makes me think of my uncle's
Shop in the country, where he has a hardware business,
Basins, pots, ewers, and alabaster birds.
He makes you die of laughing. O madam,
Isn't it sad?

[*They both weep.*

DYNAMENE

How could I have allowed you
To come and die of my grief? Doto, it puts
A terrible responsibility on me. Have you
No grief of your own you could die of?

DOTO

Not really, madam.

DYNAMENE

Nothing?

DOTO

Not really. They was all one to me.
Well, all but two was all one to me. And they,
Strange enough, was two who kept recurring.

[5]

I could never be sure if they had gone for good
Or not; and so that kept things cheerful, madam.
One always gave a wink before he deserted me,
The other slapped me as it were behind, madam;
Then they would be away for some months.

DYNAMENE

Oh Doto,
What an unhappy life you were having to lead.

DOTO

Yes, I'm sure. But never mind, madam,
It seemed quite lively then. And now I know
It's what you say; life is more big than a bed
And full of miracles and mysteries like
One man made for one woman, etcetera, etcetera.
Lovely. I feel sung, madam, by a baritone
In mixed company with everyone pleased.
And so I had to come with you here, madam,
For the last sad chorus of me. It's all
Fresh to me. Death's a new interest in life,
If it doesn't disturb you, madam, to have me crying.
It's because of us not having breakfast again.
And the master, of course. And the beautiful world.
And you crying too, madam. Oh—Oh!

DYNAMENE

I can't forbid your crying; but you must cry
On the other side of the tomb. I'm becoming confused.
This is my personal grief and my sacrifice
Of self, solus. Right over there, darling girl.

DOTO

What here?

[6]

Now, if you wish, you may cry, Doto.
But our tears are very different. For me
The world is all with Charon, all, all,
Even the metal and plume of the rose garden,
And the forest where the sea fumes overhead
In vegetable tides, and particularly
The entrance to the warm baths in Arcite Street
Where we first met;—all!—the sun itself
Trails an evening hand in the sultry river
Far away down by Acheron. I am lonely,
Virilius. Where is the punctual eye
And where is the cautious voice which made
Balance-sheets sound like Homer and Homer sound
Like balance-sheets? The precision of limbs, the amiable
Laugh, the exact festivity? Gone from the world.
You were the peroration of nature, Virilius.
You explained everything to me, even the extremely
Complicated gods. You wrote them down
In seventy columns. Dear curling calligraphy!
Gone from the world, once and for all. And I taught you
In your perceptive moments to appreciate me.
You said I was harmonious, Virilius,
Moulded and harmonious, little matronal
Ox-eye, your package. And then I would walk
Up and down largely, as it were making my own
Sunlight. What a mad blacksmith creation is
Who blows his furnaces until the stars fly upward
And iron Time is hot and politicians glow
And bulbs and roots sizzle into hyacinth
And orchis, and the sand puts out the lion,
Roaring yellow, and oceans bud with porpoises,

[8]

Blenny, tunny and the almost unexisting
Blindfish; throats are cut, the masterpiece
Looms out of labour; nations and rebellions
Are spat out to hang on the wind—and all is gone
In one Virilius, wearing his office tunic,
Checking the pence column as he went.
Where's animation now? What is there that stays
To dance? The eye of the one-eyed world is out.

> [*She weeps.*

DOTO

I shall try to grieve a little, too.
It would take lessons, I imagine, to do it out loud
For long. If I could only remember
Any one of those fellows without wanting to laugh.
Hopeless, I am. Now those good pair of shoes
I gave away without thinking, that's a different—
Well, I've cried enough about *them*, I suppose.
Poor madam, poor master.

> [TEGEUS *comes through the gate to the top of the steps.*

TEGEUS

What's your trouble?

DOTO

Oh!

Oh! Oh, a man. I thought for a moment it was something
With harm in it. Trust a man to be where it's dark.
What is it? Can't you sleep?

TEGEUS

Now, listen—

[9]

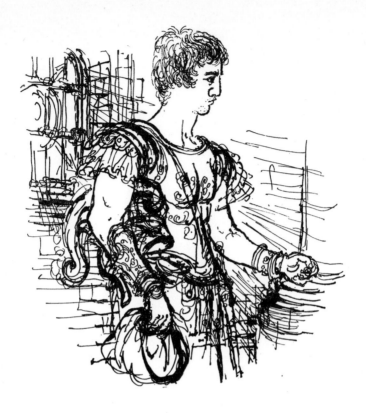

DOTO

Hush!

Remember you're in the grave. You must go away.
Madam is occupied.

TEGEUS

What, here?

DOTO

Becoming

Dead. We both are.

TEGEUS

What's going on here?

[10]

DOTO

Grief.

Are you satisfied now?

TEGEUS

Less and less. Do you know
What the time is?

DOTO

I'm not interested.
We've done with all that. Go away. Be a gentleman.
If we can't be free of men in a grave
Death's a dead loss.

TEGEUS

It's two in the morning. All
I ask is what are women doing down here
At two in the morning?

DOTO

Can't you see she's crying?
Or is she sleeping again? Either way
She's making arrangements to join her husband.

TEGEUS

Where?

DOTO

Good god, in the Underworld, dear man. Haven't you learnt
About life and death?

[11]

TEGEUS

                    In a manner, yes; in a manner;
The rudiments. So the lady means to die?

DOTO

For love; beautiful, curious madam.

TEGEUS

                              Not curious;
I've had thoughts like it. Death is a kind of love.
Not anything I can explain.

DOTO

                         You'd better come in
And sit down.

TEGEUS

I'd be grateful.

DOTO

                              Do. It will be my last
Chance to have company, in the flesh.

TEGEUS

                              Do you mean
You're going too?

DOTO

             Oh, certainly I am.
Not anything I can explain.
It all started with madam saying a man
Was two men really, and I'd only noticed one,

One each, I mean. It seems he has a soul
As well as his other troubles. And I like to know
What I'm getting with a man. I'm inquisitive,
I suppose you'd call me.

TEGEUS

It takes some courage.

DOTO

Well, yes
And no. I'm fond of change.

TEGEUS

Would you object
To have me eating my supper here?

DOTO

Be careful
Of the crumbs. We don't want a lot of squeaking mice
Just when we're dying.

TEGEUS

What a sigh she gave then.
Down the air like a slow comet.
And now she's all dark again. Mother of me.
How long has this been going on?

DOTO

Two days.
It should have been three by now, but at first
Madam had difficulty with the Town Council. They said

They couldn't have a tomb used as a private residence.
But madam told them she wouldn't be eating here,
Only suffering, and they thought that would be all right.

TEGEUS

Two of you. Marvellous. Who would have said
I should ever have stumbled on anything like this?
Do you have to cry? Yes, I suppose so. It's all
Quite reasonable.

DOTO

Your supper and your knees.
That's what's making me cry. I can't bear sympathy
And they're sympathetic.

TEGEUS

Please eat a bit of something.
I've no appetite left.

DOTO

And see her go ahead of me?
Wrap it up; put it away. You sex of wicked beards!
It's no wonder you have to shave off your black souls
Every day as they push through your chins.
I'll turn my back on you. It means utter
Contempt. Eat? Utter contempt. Oh, little new rolls!

TEGEUS

Forget it, forget it; please forget it. Remember
I've had no experience of this kind of thing before.
Indeed I'm as sorry as I know how to be. Ssh,
We'll disturb her. She sighed again. O Zeus,
It's terrible! Asleep, and still sighing.
Mourning has made a warren in her spirit,
All that way below. Ponos! the heart
Is the devil of a medicine.

DOTO

And I don't intend
To turn round.

TEGEUS

I understand how you must feel.
Would it be—have you any objection
To my having a drink? I have a little wine here.
And, you probably see how it is: grief's in order,

[15]

And death's in order, and women—I can usually
Manage that too; but not all three together
At this hour of the morning. So you'll excuse me.
How about you? It would make me more comfortable
If you'd take a smell of it.

DOTO

One for the road?

TEGEUS

One for the road.

DOTO

It's the dust in my throat. The tomb
Is so dusty. Thanks, I will. There's no point in dying
Of everything, simultaneous.

TEGEUS

It's lucky
I brought two bowls. I was expecting to keep
A drain for my relief when he comes in the morning.

DOTO

Are you on duty?

TEGEUS

Yes.

DOTO

It looks like it.

[16]

TEGEUS

Well,
Here's your good health.

DOTO

What good is that going to do me?
Here's to an easy crossing and not too much waiting
About on the bank. Do you have to tremble like that?

TEGEUS

The idea—I can't get used to it.

DOTO

For a member
Of the forces, you're peculiarly queasy. I wish
Those owls were in Hades—oh no; let them stay where they are.
Have you never had nothing to do with corpses before?

TEGEUS

I've got six of them outside.

DOTO

Morpheus, that's plenty.
What are they doing there?

TEGEUS

Hanging.

DOTO

Hanging?

TEGEUS

On trees.

Five plane trees and a holly. The holly-berries
Are just reddening. Another drink?

DOTO

Why not?

TEGEUS

It's from Samos. Here's—

DOTO

All right. Let's just drink it.
—How did they get in that predicament?

TEGEUS

The sandy-haired fellow said we should collaborate
With everybody; the little man said he wouldn't
Collaborate with anybody; the old one
Said that the Pleiades weren't sisters but cousins
And anyway were manufactured in Lacedaemon.
The fourth said that we hanged men for nothing.
The other two said nothing. Now they hang
About at the corner of the night, they're present
And absent, horribly obsequious to every
Move in the air, and yet they keep me standing
For five hours at a stretch.

DOTO

The wine has gone
Down to my knees.

[19]

And up to your cheeks. You're looking
Fresher. If only—

Madam? She never would.
Shall I ask her?

No; no, don't dare, don't breathe it.
This is privilege, to come so near
To what is undeceiving and uncorrupt
And undivided; this is the clear fashion
For all souls, a ribbon to bind the unruly
Curls of living, a faith, a hope, Zeus
Yes, a fine thing. I am human, and this
Is human fidelity, and we can be proud
And unphilosophical.

DOTO

I need to dance
But I haven't the use of my legs.

TEGEUS

No, no, don't dance,
Or, at least, only inwards; don't dance; cry
Again. We'll put a moat of tears
Round her bastion of love, and save
The world. It's something, it's more than something,
It's regeneration, to see how a human cheek
Can become as pale as a pool.

DOTO

Do you love me, handsome?

TEGEUS

To have found life, after all, unambiguous!

DOTO

Did you say Yes?

TEGEUS

Certainly; just now I love all men.

DOTO

So do I.

TEGEUS

And the world is a good creature again.
I'd begun to see it as mildew, verdigris,

Rust, woodrot, or as though the sky had uttered
An oval twirling blasphemy with occasional vistas
In country districts. I was within an ace
Of volunteering for overseas service. Despair
Abroad can always nurse pleasant thoughts of home.
Integrity, by god!

DOTO

I love all the world
And the movement of the apple in your throat.
So shall you kiss me? It would be better, I should think,
To go moistly to Hades.

TEGEUS

Her's is the way,
Luminous with sorrow.

DOTO

Then I'll take
Another little swiggy. I love all men,
Everybody, even you, and I'll pick you
Some outrageous honeysuckle for your helmet,
If only it lived here. Pardon.

DYNAMENE

Doto. Who is it?

DOTO

Honeysuckle, madam. Because of the bees.
Go back to sleep, madam.

DYNAMENE

What person is it?

DOTO

Yes, I see what you mean, madam. It's a kind of
Corporal talking to his soul, on a five-hour shift,
Madam, with six bodies. He's been having his supper.

TEGEUS

I'm going. It's terrible that we should have disturbed her.

DOTO

He was delighted to see you so sad, madam.
It has stopped him going abroad.

DYNAMENE

One with six bodies?
A messenger, a guide to where we go.
It is possible he has come to show us the way
Out of these squalid suburbs of life, a shade,
A gorgon, who has come swimming up, against
The falls of my tears (for which in truth he would need
Many limbs) to guide me to Virilius.
I shall go quietly.

TEGEUS

I do assure you—
Such clumsiness, such a vile and unforgivable
Intrusion. I shall obliterate myself
Immediately.

[23]

DOTO

Oblit—oh, what a pity
To oblit. Pardon. Don't let him, the nice fellow.

DYNAMENE

Sir: your other five bodies: where are they?

TEGEUS

                                    Madam—

Outside; I have them outside. On trees.

DYNAMENE

                        Quack!

TEGEUS

What do I reply?

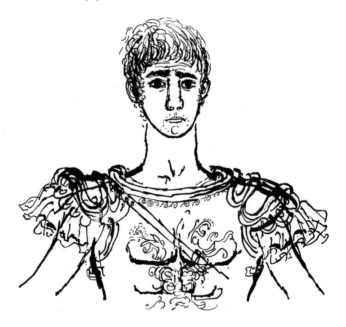

DYNAMENE

       Quack, charlatan!
You've never known the gods. You came to mock me.
Doto, this never was a gorgon, never.
Nor a gentleman either. He's completely spurious.
Admit it, you creature. Have you even a feather
Of the supernatural in your system? Have you?

TEGEUS

Some of my relations—

DYNAMENE

       Well?

TEGEUS

                 Are dead, I think;
That is to say I have connexions—

DYNAMENE

               Connexions
With pickpockets. It's a shameless imposition.
Does the army provide you with no amusements?
If I were still of the world, and not cloistered
In a colourless landscape of winter thought
Where the approaching Spring is desired oblivion,
I should write sharply to your commanding officer.
It should be done, it should be done. If my fingers
Weren't so cold I would do it now. But they are,

[25]

Horribly cold. And why should insolence matter
When my colour of life is unreal, a blush on death,
A partial mere diaphane? I don't know
Why it should matter. Oafish, non-commissioned
Young man! The boots of your conscience will pinch for ever
If life's dignity has any self-protection.
Oh, I have to sit down. The tomb's going round.

DOTO

Oh, madam, don't give over. I can't remember
When things were so lively. He looks marvellously
Marvellously uncomfortable. Go on, madam.
Can't you, madam? Oh, madam, don't you feel up to it?
There, do you see her, you acorn-chewing infantryman?
You've made her cry, you square-bashing barbarian.

TEGEUS

O history, my private history, why
Was I led here? What stigmatism has got
Into my stars? Why wasn't it my brother?
He has a tacit misunderstanding with everybody
And washes in it. Why wasn't it my mother?
She makes a collection of other people's tears
And dries them all. Let them forget I came;
And lie in the terrible black crystal of grief
Which held them, before I broke it. Outside, Tegeus.

DOTO

Hey, I don't think so, I shouldn't say so. Come
Down again, uniform. Do you think you're going

To half kill an unprotected lady and then
Back out upwards? Do you think you can leave her like this?

TEGEUS

Yes, yes, I'll leave her. O directorate of gods,
How can I? Beauty's bit is between my teeth.
She has added another torture to me. Bottom
Of Hades' bottom.

DOTO

                    Madam. Madam, the corporal
Has some wine here. It will revive you, madam.
And then you can go at him again, madam.

TEGEUS

It's the opposite of everything you've said,
I swear, I swear by Horkos and the Styx,
I swear by the nine acres of Tityos,
I swear the Hypnotic oath, by all the Titans—
By Koeos, Krios, Iapetos, Kronos, and so on—
By the three Hekatoncheires, by the insomnia
Of Tisiphone, by Jove, by jove, and the dew
On the feet of my boyhood, I am innocent
Of mocking you. Am I a Salmoneus
That, seeing such a flame of sorrow—

DYNAMENE

                              You needn't
Labour to prove your secondary education.
Perhaps I jumped to a wrong conclusion, perhaps
I was hasty.

[27]

DOTO

How easy to swear if you're properly educated.
Wasn't it pretty, madam? Pardon.

DYNAMENE

If I misjudged you
I apologize, I apologize. Will you please leave us?
You were wrong to come here. In a place of mourning
Light itself is a trespasser; nothing can have
The right of entrance except those natural symbols
Of mortality, the jabbing, funeral, sleek-
With-omen raven, the death-watch beetle which mocks
Time: particularly, I'm afraid, the spider
Weaving his home with swift self-generated
Threads of slaughter; and, of course, the worm.
I wish it could be otherwise. Oh dear,
They aren't easy to live with.

DOTO

Not even a *little* wine, madam?

DYNAMENE

Here, Doto?

DOTO

Well, on the steps perhaps,
Except it's so draughty.

DYNAMENE

Doto! Here?

[28]

DOTO

No, madam;
I quite see.

DYNAMENE

I might be wise to strengthen myself
In order to fast again; it would make me abler
For grief. I will breathe a little of it, Doto.

DOTO

Thank god. Where's the bottle?

DYNAMENE

What an exquisite bowl.

TEGEUS

Now that it's peacetime we have pottery classes.

DYNAMENE

You made it yourself?

TEGEUS

Yes. Do you see the design?
The corded god, tied also by the rays
Of the sun, and the astonished ship erupting
Into vines and vine-leaves, inverted pyramids
Of grapes, the uplifted hands of the men (the raiders),
And here the headlong sea, itself almost
Venturing into leaves and tendrils, and Proteus
With his beard braiding the wind, and this
Held by other hands is a drowned sailor—

[30]

DYNAMENE

Always, always.

DOTO

Hold the bowl steady, madam.
Pardon.

DYNAMENE

Doto, have you been drinking?

DOTO

Here, madam?
I coaxed some a little way towards my mouth, madam,
But I scarcely swallowed except because I had to. The hiccup
Is from no breakfast, madam, and not meant to be funny.

DYNAMENE

You may drink this too. Oh, how the inveterate body,
Even when cut from the heart, insists on leaf,
Puts out, with a separate meaningless will,
Fronds to intercept the thankless sun.
How it does, oh, how it does. And how it confuses
The nature of the mind.

TEGEUS

Yes, yes, the confusion;
That's something I understand better than anything.

[31]

DYNAMENE

When the thoughts would die, the instincts will set sail
For life. And when the thoughts are alert for life
The instincts will rage to be destroyed on the rocks.
To Virilius it was not so; his brain was an ironing-board
For all crumpled indecision: and I follow him,
The hawser of my world. You don't belong here,
You see; you don't belong here at all.

TEGEUS

                                        If only
I did. If only you knew the effort it costs me
To mount those steps again into an untrustworthy,
Unpredictable, unenlightened night,
And turn my back on—on a state of affairs,
I can only call it a vision, a hope, a promise,
A— By that I mean loyalty, enduring passion,
Unrecking bravery and beauty all in one.

DOTO

He means you, or you and me; or me, madam.

TEGEUS

It only remains for me to thank you, and to say
That whatever awaits me and for however long
I may be played by this poor musician, existence,
Your person and sacrifice will leave their trace
As clear upon me as the shape of the hills
Around my birthplace. Now I must leave you to your husband.

DOTO

Oh! You, madam.

DYNAMENE

I'll tell you what I will do.
I will drink with you to the memory of my husband,
Because I have been curt, because you are kind,
And because I'm extremely thirsty. And then we will say
Good-bye and part to go to our opposite corruptions,
The world and the grave.

TEGEUS

The climax to the vision.

DYNAMENE [*drinking*]

My husband, and all he stood for.

TEGEUS

Stands for.

DYNAMENE

Stands for.

TEGEUS

Your husband.

DOTO

The master.

DYNAMENE

How good it is,
How it sings to the throat, purling with summer.

TEGEUS

It has a twin nature, winter and warmth in one,
Moon and meadow. Do you agree?

DYNAMENE

Perfectly;
A cold bell sounding in a golden month.

TEGEUS

Crystal in harvest.

DYNAMENE

Perhaps a nightingale
Sobbing among the pears.

TEGEUS

In an old autumnal midnight.

DOTO

Grapes.—Pardon. There's some more here.

TEGEUS

Plenty.

I drink to the memory of your husband.

DYNAMENE

My husband.

DOTO

The master.

DYNAMENE

He was careless in his choice of wines.

TEGEUS

And yet

Rendering to living its rightful poise is not
Unimportant.

DYNAMENE

A mystery's in the world
Where a little liquid, with flavour, quality, and fume
Can be as no other, can hint and flute our senses
As though a music played in harvest hollows
And a movement was in the swathes of our memory.
Why should scent, why should flavour come
With such wings upon us? Parsley, for instance.

TEGEUS

Seaweed.

DYNAMENE

Lime trees.

DOTO

Horses.

TEGEUS

Fruit in the fire.

DYNAMENE

Do I know your name?

TEGEUS

Tegeus.

DYNAMENE

That's very thin for you,
It hardly covers your bones. Something quite different,
Altogether other. I shall think of it presently.

TEGEUS

Darker vowels, perhaps.

DYNAMENE

Yes, certainly darker vowels.
And your consonants should have a slight angle,
And a certain temperature. Do you know what I mean?
It will come to me.

[36]

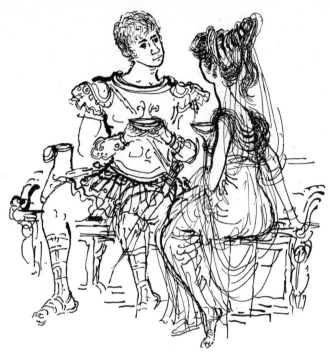

TEGEUS

Now *your* name—

DYNAMENE

It is nothing
To any purpose. I'll be to you the She
In the tomb. You have the air of a natural-historian
As though you were accustomed to handling birds' eggs,
Or tadpoles, or putting labels on moths. You see?
The genius of dumb things, that they are nameless.
Have I found the seat of the weevil in human brains?
Our names. They make us broody; we sit and sit
To hatch them into reputation and dignity.
And then they set upon us and become despair,
Guilt and remorse. We go where they lead. We dance

Attendance on something wished upon us by the wife
Of our mother's physician. But insects meet and part
And put the woods about them, fill the dusk
And freckle the light and go and come without
A name among them, without the wish of a name
And very pleasant too. Did I interrupt you?

TEGEUS

I forget. We'll have no names then.

DYNAMENE

                                I should like
You to have a name, I don't know why; a small one
To fill out the conversation.

TEGEUS

                        I should like
You to have a name too, if only for something
To remember. Have you still some wine in your bowl?

DYNAMENE

Not altogether.

TEGEUS

                        We haven't come to the end
By several inches. Did I splash you?

DYNAMENE

                                It doesn't matter.
Well, here's to my husband's name.

TEGEUS

Your husband's name.

DOTO

The master.

DYNAMENE

It was kind of you to come.

TEGEUS

It was more than coming. I followed my future here,
As we all do if we're sufficiently inattentive
And don't vex ourselves with questions; or do I mean
Attentive? If so, attentive to what? Do I sound
Incoherent?

DYNAMENE

You're wrong. There isn't a future here,
Not here, not for you.

TEGEUS

Your name's Dynamene.

DYNAMENE

Who—Have I been utterly irreverent? Are you—
Who made you say that? Forgive me the question,
But are you dark or light? I mean which shade
Of the supernatural? Or if neither, what prompted you?

TEGEUS

Dynamene——

[39]

DYNAMENE

No, but I'm sure you're the friend of nature,
It must be so, I think I see little Phoebuses
Rising and setting in your eyes.

DOTO

They're not little Phoebuses,
They're hoodwinks, madam. Your name is on your brooch.
No little Phoebuses to-night.

DYNAMENE

That's twice
You've played me a trick. Oh, I know practical jokes
Are common on Olympus, but haven't we at all
Developed since the gods were born? Are gods
And men both to remain immortal adolescents?
How tiresome it all is.

TEGEUS

It was you, each time,
Who said I was supernatural. When did I say so?
You're making me into whatever you imagine
And then you blame me because I can't live up to it.

DYNAMENE

I shall call you Chromis. It has a breadlike sound.
I think of you as a crisp loaf.

TEGEUS

And now
You'll insult me because I'm not sliceable.

[40]

DYNAMENE

I think drinking is harmful to our tempers.

TEGEUS

If I seem to be frowning, that is only because
I'm looking directly into your light: I must look
Angrily, or shut my eyes.

DYNAMENE

                    Shut them.—Oh,
You have eyelashes! A new perspective of you.
Is that how you look when you sleep?

TEGEUS

                                        My jaw drops down.

DYNAMENE

Show me how.

TEGEUS

        Like this.

DYNAMENE

                    It makes an irresistible
Moron of you. Will you waken now?
It's morning; I see a thin dust of daylight
Blowing on to the steps.

TEGEUS

                Already? Dynamene,
You're tricked again. This time by the moon.

[42]

DYNAMENE

Oh well,
Moon's daylight, then. Doto is asleep.

TEGEUS

Doto
Is asleep . . .

DYNAMENE

Chromis, what made you walk about
In the night? What, I wonder, made you not stay
Sleeping wherever you slept? Was it the friction
Of the world on your mind? Those two are difficult
To make agree. Chromis—now try to learn
To answer your name. I won't say Tegeus.

TEGEUS

And I
Won't say Dynamene.

DYNAMENE

Not?

TEGEUS

It makes you real.
Forgive me, a terrible thing has happened. Shall I
Say it and perhaps destroy myself for you?
Forgive me first, or, more than that, forgive
Nature who winds her furtive stream all through
Our reason. Do you forgive me?

[43]

DYNAMENE

                        I'll forgive
Anything, if it's the only way I can know
What you have to tell me.

TEGEUS

                    I felt us to be alone;
Here in a grave, separate from any life,
I and the only one of beauty, the only
Persuasive key to all my senses,
In spite of my having lain day after day
And pored upon the sepals, corolla, stamen, and bracts
Of the yellow bog-iris. Then my body ventured
A step towards interrupting your perfection of purpose
And my own renewed faith in human nature.
Would you have believed that possible?

DYNAMENE

                        I have never
Been greatly moved by the yellow bog-iris. Alas,
It's as I said. This place is for none but the spider,
Raven and worms, not for a living man.

TEGEUS

It has been a place of blessing to me. It will always
Play in me, a fountain of confidence
When the world is arid. But I know it is true
I have to leave it, and though it withers my soul
I must let you make your journey.

DYNAMENE

                No.

TEGEUS

Not true?

DYNAMENE

We can talk of something quite different.

TEGEUS

Yes, we can!

Oh yes, we will! Is it your opinion
That no one believes who hasn't learned to doubt?
Or, another thing, if we persuade ourselves
To one particular Persuasion, become Sophist,
Stoic, Platonist, anything whatever,
Would you say that there must be areas of soul
Lying unproductive therefore, or dishonoured
Or blind?

DYNAMENE

No, I don't know.

TEGEUS

No. It's impossible
To tell. Dynamene, if only I had
Two cakes of pearl-barley and hydromel
I could see you to Hades, leave you with your husband
And come back to the world.

DYNAMENE

Ambition, I suppose,
Is an appetite particular to man.
What is your definition?

TEGEUS

The desire to find
A reason for living.

DYNAMENE

But then, suppose it leads,
As often, one way or another, it does, to death.

TEGEUS

Then that may be life's reason. Oh, but how
Could I bear to return, Dynamene? The earth's
Daylight would be my grave if I had left you
In that unearthly night.

DYNAMENE

O Chromis——

TEGEUS

Tell me,
What is your opinion of Progress? Does it, for example,
Exist? Is there ever progression without retrogression?
Therefore is it not true that mankind
Can more justly be said increasingly to Gress?
As the material improves, the craftsmanship deteriorates
And honour and virtue remain the same. I love you,
Dynamene.

DYNAMENE

Would you consider we go round and round?

TEGEUS

We concertina, I think; taking each time
A larger breath, so that the farther we go out
The farther we have to go in.

DYNAMENE

There'll come a time
When it will be unbearable to continue.

TEGEUS

Unbearable.

DYNAMENE

Perhaps we had better have something
To eat. The wine has made your eyes so quick
I am breathless beside them. It *is*
Your eyes, I think; or your intelligence

Holding my intelligence up above you
Between its hands. Or the cut of your uniform.

TEGEUS

Here's a new roll with honey. In the gods' names
Let's sober ourselves.

DYNAMENE

As soon as possible.

TEGEUS

Have you
Any notion of algebra?

DYNAMENE

We'll discuss you, Chromis.
We will discuss you, till you're nothing but words.

TEGEUS

I? There is nothing, of course, I would rather discuss,
Except—if it would be no intrusion—you, Dynamene.

DYNAMENE

No, you couldn't want to. But your birthplace, Chromis,
With the hills that placed themselves in you for ever
As you say, where was it?

TEGEUS

My father's farm at Pyxa.

DYNAMENE

There? Could it be there?

TEGEUS

I was born in the hills
Between showers, a quarter of an hour before milking time.
Do you know Pyxa? It stretches to the crossing of two
Troublesome roads, and buries its back in beechwood,
From which come the white owls of our nights
And the mulling and cradling of doves in the day.
I attribute my character to those shadows
And heavy roots; and my interest in music
To the sudden melodious escape of the young river
Where it breaks from nosing through the cresses and kingcups.
That's honestly so.

DYNAMENE

You used to climb about
Among the windfallen tower of Phrasidemus
Looking for bees' nests.

TEGEUS

What? When have I
Said so?

DYNAMENE

Why, all the children did.

TEGEUS

Yes: but, in the name of light, how do you *know* that?

DYNAMENE

I played there once, on holiday.

TEGEUS

                    O Klotho,
Lachesis and Atropos!

DYNAMENE

                It's the strangest chance:
I may have seen, for a moment, your boyhood.

TEGEUS

                                    I may
Have seen something like an early flower
Something like a girl. If I only could remember how I must

Have seen you. Were you after the short white violets?
Maybe I blundered past you, taking your look,
And scarcely acknowledged how a star
Ran through me, to live in the brooks of my blood for ever.
Or I saw you playing at hiding in the cave
Where the ferns are and the water drips.

DYNAMENE

I was quite plain and fat and I was usually
Hitting someone. I wish I could remember you.
I'm envious of the days and children who saw you
Then. It is curiously a little painful
Not to share your past.

TEGEUS

How did it come
Our stars could mingle for an afternoon
So long ago, and then forget us or tease us
Or helplessly look on the dark high seas
Of our separation, while time drank
The golden hours? What hesitant fate is that?

DYNAMENE

Time? Time? Why—how old are we?

TEGEUS

Young,
Thank both our mothers, but still we're older than to-night
And so older than we should be. Wasn't I born
In love with what, only now, I have grown to meet?
I'll tell you something else. I was born entirely

[51]

For this reason. I was born to fill a gap
In the world's experience, which had never known
Chromis loving Dynamene.

DYNAMENE

You are so
Excited, poor Chromis. What is it? Here you sit
With a woman who has wept away all claims
To appearance, unbecoming in her oldest clothes,
With not a trace of liveliness, a drab
Of melancholy, entirely shadow without
A smear of sun. Forgive me if I tell you
That you fall easily into superlatives.

TEGEUS

Very well. I'll say nothing, then. I'll fume
With feeling.

DYNAMENE

Now you go to the extreme. Certainly
You must speak. You may have more to say. Besides
You might let your silence run away with you
And not say something that you should. And how
Should I answer you then? Chromis, you boy,
I can't look away from you. You use
The lamplight and the moon so skilfully,
So arrestingly, in and around your furrows.
A humorous ploughman goes whistling to a team
Of sad sorrow, to and fro in your brow
And over your arable cheek. Laugh for me. Have you
Cried for women, ever?

TEGEUS

        In looking about for you.
But I have recognized them for what they were.

DYNAMENE

What are they?

TEGEUS

        Never you: never, although
They could walk with bright distinction into all men's
Longest memories, never you, by a hint
Or a faint quality, or at least not more
Than reflectively, stars lost and uncertain
In the sea, compared with the shining salt, the shiners,
The galaxies, the clusters, the bright grain whirling
Over the black threshing-floor of space.
Will you make some effort to believe that?

DYNAMENE

                No, no effort.
It lifts me and carries me. It may be wild
But it comes to me with a charm, like trust indeed,
And eats out of my heart, dear Chromis,
Absurd, disconcerting Chromis. You make me
Feel I wish I could look my best for you.
I wish, at least, that I could believe myself
To be showing some beauty for you, to put in the scales
Between us. But they dip to you, they sink
With masculine victory.

[53]

TEGEUS

Eros, no! No!
If this is less than your best, then never, in my presence,
Be more than your less: never! If you should bring
More to your mouth or to your eyes, a moisture
Or a flake of light, anything, anything fatally
More, perfection would fetch her unsparing rod
Out of pickle to flay me, and what would have been love
Will be the end of me. O Dynamene,
Let me unload something of my lips' longing
On to yours receiving. Oh, when I cross
Like this the hurt of the little space between us
I come a journey from the wrenching ice
To walk in the sun. That is the feeling.

DYNAMENE

Chromis,
Where am I going? No, don't answer. It's death
I desire, not you.

TEGEUS

Where is the difference? Call me
Death instead of Chromis. I'll answer to anything.
It's desire all the same, of death in me, or me
In death, but Chromis either way. Is it so?
Do you not love me, Dynamene?

DYNAMENE

How could it happen?
I'm going to my husband. I'm too far on the way
To admit myself to life again. Love's in Hades.

Also here. And here are we, not there
In Hades. Is your husband expecting you?

Surely, surely?

Not necessarily. I,
If I had been your husband, would never dream
Of expecting you. I should remember your body
Descending stairs in the floating light, but not
Descending in Hades. I should say 'I have left
My wealth warm on the earth, and, hell, earth needs it.'
'Was all I taught her of love,' I should say, 'so poor
That she will leave her flesh and become shadow?'
'Wasn't our love for each other' (I should continue)
'Infused with life, and life infused with our love?
Very well; repeat me in love, repeat me in life,
And let me sing in your blood for ever.'

Stop, stop, I shall be dragged apart!
Why should the fates do everything to keep me
From dying honourably? They must have got
Tired of honour in Elysium. Chromis, it's terrible
To be susceptible to two conflicting norths.
I have the constitution of a whirlpool.
Am I actually twirling, or is it just sensation?

You're still; still as the darkness.

DYNAMENE

What appears
Is so unlike what is. And what is madness
To those who only observe, is often wisdom
To those to whom it happens.

TEGEUS

Are we compelled
To go into all this?

DYNAMENE

Why, how could I return
To my friends? Am I to be an entertainment?

TEGEUS

That's for to-morrow. To-night I need to kiss you,
Dynamene. Let's see what the whirlpool does
Between my arms; let it whirl on my breast. O love,
Come in.

DYNAMENE

I am there before I reach you; my body
Only follows to join my longing which
Is holding you already.—Now I am
All one again.

TEGEUS

I feel as the gods feel:
This is their sensation of life, not a man's:
Their suspension of immortality, to enrich
Themselves with time. O life, O death, O body,
O spirit, O Dynamene.

[57]

DYNAMENE

O all

In myself; it so covets all in you,
My care, my Chromis. Then I shall be
Creation.

TEGEUS

You have the skies already;
Out of them you are buffeting me with your gales
Of beauty. Can we be made of dust, as they tell us?
What! dust with dust releasing such a light
And such an apparition of the world
Within one body? A thread of your hair has stung me.
Why do you push me away?

DYNAMENE

There's so much metal
About you. Do I have to be imprisoned
In an armoury?

TEGEUS

Give your hand to the buckles and then
To me.

DYNAMENE

Don't help; I'll do them all myself.

TEGEUS

O time and patience! I want you back again.

DYNAMENE

We have a lifetime. O Chromis, think, think
Of that. And even unfastening a buckle
Is loving. And not easy. Very well,
You can help me. Chromis, what zone of miracle
Did you step into to direct you in the dark
To where I waited, not knowing I waited?

TEGEUS

                                                    I saw
The lamplight. That was only the appearance
Of some great gesture in the bed of fortune.
I saw the lamplight.

DYNAMENE

But here ? So far from life ?
What brought you near enough to see lamplight ?

TEGEUS

Zeus,
That reminds me.

DYNAMENE

What is it, Chromis ?

TEGEUS

I'm on duty.

DYNAMENE

Is it warm enough to do without your greaves ?

TEGEUS

Darling loom of magic, I must go back
To take a look at those boys. The whole business
Of guard had gone out of my mind.

DYNAMENE

What boys, my heart ?

TEGEUS

My six bodies.

DYNAMENE

Chromis, not that joke
Again.

TEGEUS

No joke, sweet. To-day our city
Held a sextuple hanging. I'm minding the bodies
Until five o'clock. Already I've been away
For half an hour.

DYNAMENE

What can they do, poor bodies,
In half an hour, or half a century?
You don't really mean to go?

TEGEUS

Only to make
My conscience easy. Then, Dynamene,
No cloud can rise on love, no hovering thought
Fidget, and the night will be only to *us*.

DYNAMENE

But if every half-hour——

TEGEUS

Hush, smile of my soul,
My sprig, my sovereign: this is to hold your eyes,
I sign my lips on them both: this is to keep
Your forehead—do you feel the claim of my kiss
Falling into your thought? And now your throat
Is a white branch and my lips two singing birds—
They are coming to rest. Throat, remember me
Until I come back in five minutes. Over all
Here is my parole: I give it to your mouth
To give me again before it's dry. I promise:
Before it's dry, or not long after.

DYNAMENE

Run,
Run all the way. You needn't be afraid of stumbling.
There's plenty of moon. The fields are blue. Oh, wait,
Wait! My darling. No, not now: it will keep
Until I see you; I'll have it here at my lips.
Hurry.

TEGEUS

So long, my haven.

DYNAMENE

Hurry, hurry!

[*Exit* TEGEUS.

Yes, madam, hurry; of course. Are we there
Already? How nice. Death doesn't take
Any doing at all. We were gulped into Hades
As easy as an oyster.

DYNAMENE

Doto!

DOTO

Hurry, hurry,
Yes, madam.—But they've taken out all my bones.
I haven't a bone left. I'm a Shadow: wonderfully shady
In the legs. We shall have to sit out eternity, madam,
If they've done the same to you.

DYNAMENE

You'd better wake up.
If you can't go to sleep again, you'd better wake up.
Oh dear.—We're still alive, Doto, do you hear me?

DOTO

You must speak for yourself, madam. I'm quite dead.
I'll tell you how I know. I feel
Invisible. I'm a wraith, madam; I'm only
Waiting to be wafted.

DYNAMENE

If only you *would* be.
Do you see where you are? Look. Do you see?

DOTO

Yes. You're right, madam. We're still alive.
Isn't it enough to make you swear?
Here we are, dying to be dead,
And where does it get us?

DYNAMENE

                    Perhaps you should try to die
In some other place. Yes! Perhaps the air here
Suits you too well. You were sleeping very heavily.

DOTO

And all the time you alone and dying.
I shouldn't have. Has the corporal been long gone,
Madam?

DYNAMENE

        He came and went, came and went,
You know the way.

DOTO

            Very well I do. And went
He should have, come he should never. Oh dear, he must
Have disturbed you, madam.

DYNAMENE

                He could be said
To've disturbed me. Listen; I have something to say to you.

DOTO

I expect so, madam. Maybe I *could* have kept him out
But men are in before I wish they wasn't.
I think quickly enough, but I get behindhand
With what I ought to be saying. It's a kind of stammer
In my way of life, madam.

DYNAMENE

I have been unkind,
I have sinfully wronged you, Doto.

DOTO

Never, madam.

DYNAMENE

Oh yes. I was letting you die with me, Doto, without
Any fair reason. I was drowning you
In grief that wasn't yours. That was wrong, Doto.

DOTO

But I haven't got anything against dying, madam.
I may *like* the situation, as far as I like
Any situation, madam. Now if you'd said mangling,
A lot of mangling, I might have thought twice about staying.
We all have our dislikes, madam.

DYNAMENE

I'm asking you
To leave me, Doto, at once, as quickly as possible,
Now, before—now, Doto, and let me forget

My bad mind which confidently expected you
To companion me to Hades. Now good-bye,
Good-bye.

DOTO

No, it's not good-bye at all.
I shouldn't know another night of sleep, wondering
How you got on, or what I was missing, come to that.
I should be anxious about you, too. When you belong
To an upper class, the netherworld might come strange.
Now I was born nether, madam, though not
As nether as some. No, it's not good-bye, madam.

DYNAMENE

Oh Doto, go; you must, you must! And if I seem
Without gratitude, forgive me. It isn't so,
It is far, far from so. But I can only
Regain my peace of mind if I know you're gone.

DOTO

Besides, look at the time, madam. Where should I go
At three in the morning? Even if I was to think
Of going; and think of it I never shall.

DYNAMENE

Think of the unmatchable world, Doto.

DOTO

I do
Think of it, madam. And when I think of it, what
Have I thought? Well, it depends, madam.

[66]

DYNAMENE

I insist,

Obey me! At once! Doto!

DOTO

Here I sit.

DYNAMENE

What shall I do with you?

DOTO

Ignore me, madam.
I know my place. I shall die quite unobtrusive.
Oh look, the corporal's forgotten to take his equipment.

DYNAMENE

Could he be so careless?

DOTO

I shouldn't hardly have thought so.
Poor fellow. They'll go and deduct it off his credits.
I suppose, madam, I suppose he couldn't be thinking
Of coming back?

DYNAMENE

He'll think of these. He will notice
He isn't wearing them. He'll come; he is sure to come.

DOTO

Oh.

DYNAMENE

I know he will.

DOTO

Oh, oh.
Is that all for to-night, madam? May I go now, madam?

DYNAMENE

Doto! Will you?

DOTO

Just you try to stop me, madam.
Sometimes going is a kind of instinct with me.
I'll leave death to some other occasion.

DYNAMENE

Do,
Doto. Any other time. Now you must hurry.
I won't delay you from life another moment.
Oh, Doto, good-bye.

DOTO

Good-bye. Life is unusual,
Isn't it, madam? Remember me to Cerberus.
                    [*Re-enter* TEGEUS. DOTO *passes him on the steps.*

DOTO [*as she goes*]
You left something behind. Ye gods, what a moon!

DYNAMENE

Chromis, it's true; my lips are hardly dry.
Time runs again; the void is space again;
Space has life again; Dynamene has Chromis.

TEGEUS

It's over.

DYNAMENE

      Chromis, you're sick. As white as wool.
Come, you covered the distance too quickly.
Rest in my arms; get your breath again.

TEGEUS

I've breathed one night too many. Why did I see you,
Why in the name of life did I see you?

DYNAMENE

                        Why?
Weren't we gifted with each other? O heart,
What do you mean?

TEGEUS

                I mean that joy is nothing
But the parent of doom. Why should I have found
Your constancy such balm to the world and yet
Find, by the same vision, its destruction
A necessity? We're set upon by love
To make us incompetent to steer ourselves,
To make us docile to fate. I should have known:
Indulgences, not fulfilment, is what the world
Permits us.

Chromis, is this intelligible?
Help me to follow you. What did you meet in the fields
To bring about all this talk? Do you still love me?

TEGEUS

What good will it do us? I've lost a body.

DYNAMENE

A body?
One of the six? Well, it isn't with them you propose
To love me; and you couldn't keep it for ever.
Are we going to allow a body that isn't there
To come between us?

TEGEUS

                  But I'm responsible for it.
I have to account for it in the morning. Surely
You see, Dynamene, the horror we're faced with?
The relatives have had time to cut him down
And take him away for burial. It means
A court martial. No doubt about the sentence.
I shall take the place of the missing man.
To be hanged, Dynamene! Hanged, Dynamene!

DYNAMENE

No; it's monstrous! Your life is yours, Chromis.

TEGEUS

Anything but. That's why I have to take it.
At the best we live our lives on loan,
At the worst in chains. And I was never born
To have life. Then for what? To be had by it,
And so are we all. But I'll make it what it is,
By making it nothing.

DYNAMENE

                 Chromis, you're frightening me.
What are you meaning to do?

TEGEUS

                 I have to die,
Dance of my heart, I have to die, to die,
To part us, to go to my sword and let it part us.
I'll have my free will even if I'm compelled to it.
I'll kill myself.

[72]

DYNAMENE

Oh, no! No, Chromis!
It's all unreasonable—no such horror
Can come of a pure accident. Have you hanged?
How can they hang you for simply not being somewhere?
How can they hang you for losing a dead man?
They must have wanted to lose him, or they wouldn't
Have hanged him. No, you're scaring yourself for nothing
And making me frantic.

TEGEUS

It's section six, paragraph
Three in the Regulations. That's my doom.
I've read it for myself. And, by my doom,
Since I have to die, let me die here, in love,
Promoted by your kiss to tower, in dying,
High above my birth. For god's sake let me die
On a wave of life, Dynamene, with an action
I can take some pride in. How could I settle to death
Knowing that you last saw me stripped and strangled
On a holly tree? Demoted first and then hanged!

DYNAMENE

Am I supposed to love the corporal
Or you? It's you I love, from head to foot
And out to the ends of your spirit. What shall I do
If you die? How could I follow you? I should find you
Discussing me with my husband, comparing your feelings,
Exchanging reactions. Where should I put myself?
Or am I to live on alone, or find in life
Another source of love, in memory
Of Virilius and of you?

[73]

TEGEUS

Dynamene,
Not that! Since everything in the lives of men
Is brief to indifference, let our love at least
Echo and perpetuate itself uniquely
As long as time allows you. Though you go
To the limit of age, it won't be far to contain me.

DYNAMENE

It will seem like eternity ground into days and days.

TEGEUS

Can I be certain of you, for ever?

DYNAMENE

But, Chromis,
Surely you said——

TEGEUS

Surely we have sensed
Our passion to be greater than mortal? Must I
Die believing it is dying with me?

DYNAMENE

Chromis,
You must never die, never! It would be
An offence against truth.

TEGEUS

I cannot live to be hanged.
It would be an offence against life. Give me my sword,

Dynamene. O Hades, when you look pale
You take the heart out of me. I could die
Without a sword by seeing you suffer. Quickly!
Give me my heart back again with your lips
And I'll live the rest of my ambitions
In a last kiss.

DYNAMENE

       Oh, no, no, no!
Give my blessing to your desertion of me?
Never, Chromis, never. Kiss you and then
Let you go? Love you, for death to have you?
Am I to be made the fool of courts martial?
Who are they who think they can discipline souls
Right off the earth? What discipline is that?
Chromis, love is the only discipline
And we're the disciples of love. I hold you to that:
Hold you, hold you.

TEGEUS

　　　　　We have no chance. It's determined
In section six, paragraph three, of the Regulations.
That has more power than love. It can snuff the great
Candles of creation. It makes me able
To do the impossible, to leave you, to go from the light
That keeps you.

DYNAMENE

　　　No!

TEGEUS

　　　　　O dark, it does. Good-bye,
My memory of earth, my dear most dear
Beyond every expectation. I was wrong
To want you to keep our vows existent
In the vacuum that's coming. It would make you
A heaviness to the world, when you should be,
As you are, a form of light. Dynamene, turn
Your head away. I'm going to let my sword
Solve all the riddles.

DYNAMENE

　　　　Chromis, I have it! I know!
Virilius will help you.

TEGEUS

　　　Virilius?

DYNAMENE

My husband. He can be the other body.

[76]

Your husband can?

DYNAMENE

He has no further use
For what he left of himself to lie with us here.
Is there any reason why he shouldn't hang
On your holly tree? Better, far better, he,
Than you who are still alive, and surely better
Than *idling* into corruption?

TEGEUS

Hang your husband?
Dynamene, it's terrible, horrible.

DYNAMENE

How little you can understand. I loved
His life not his death. And now we can give his death
The power of life. Not horrible: wonderful!
Isn't it so? That I should be able to feel
He moves again in the world, accomplishing
Our welfare? It's more than my grief could do.

TEGEUS

What can I say?

DYNAMENE

That you love me; as I love him
And you. Let's celebrate your safety then.
Where's the bottle? There's some wine unfinished in this bowl.

[77]

I'll share it with you. Now forget the fear
We were in; look at me, Chromis. Come away
From the pit you nearly dropped us in. My darling,
I give you Virilius.

TEGEUS

Virilius.
And all that follows.

DOTO [*on the steps*, *with the bottle*]
The master. Both the masters.

CURTAIN

PRINTED IN GREAT BRITAIN
AT THE UNIVERSITY PRESS, OXFORD
BY VIVIAN RIDLER
PRINTER TO THE UNIVERSITY